Set design by George Xenos and Dorothea Brunialti   *Photo by Dorothea Brunialti*

The set of the New York production of *Summer Cyclone*.

SUMMER CYCLONE

BY AMY FOX

DRAMATISTS
PLAY SERVICE
INC.

NOTE ON BILLING

Anyone receiving permission to produce SUMMER CYCLONE is required to give credit to the Author as sole and exclusive Author of the Play on the title page of all programs distributed in connection with performances of the Play and in all instances in which the title of the Play appears, including printed or digital materials for advertising, publicizing or otherwise exploiting the Play and/or a production thereof. The name of the Author must appear on a separate line, in which no other name appears, immediately beneath the title and in size of type equal to 50% of the size of the largest, most prominent letter used for the title of the Play. No person, firm or entity may receive credit larger or more prominent than the Author. The following acknowledgment must appear on the title page in all programs distributed in connection with performances of the Play:

Summer Cyclone was originally produced by
The Ensemble Studio Theatre and Youngblood
in association with Watermark Theatre on February 21, 2001
at The Ensemble Studio Theatre, New York City.

SPECIAL NOTE ON SONGS/RECORDINGS

Dramatists Play Service neither holds the rights to nor grants permission to use any songs or recordings mentioned in the Play. Permission for performances of copyrighted songs, arrangements or recordings mentioned in this Play is not included in our license agreement. The permission of the copyright owner(s) must be obtained for any such use. For any songs and/or recordings mentioned in the Play, other songs, arrangements, or recordings may be substituted provided permission from the copyright owner(s) of such songs, arrangements or recordings is obtained; or songs, arrangements or recordings in the public domain may be substituted.

SUMMER CYCLONE was originally produced by The Ensemble Studio Theatre (Curt Dempster, Artistic Director; Jamie Richards, Executive Producer; Eliza Beckwith, Managing Director) in association with Youngblood (Chris Smith, Artistic Director) in New York City on February 21, 2001. It was directed by Nela Wagman; the set design was by George Xenos and Dorothea Brunialti; the lighting design was by Greg MacPherson; the sound design was by Dean Gray; the composer was David Rothenberg; the costume design was by Amela Baksic; and the stage manager was Carolyn M. Bennett. The cast was as follows:

LUCIA .... Jenna Stern
JULIET .... Christine Farrell
JEREMY .... Chris Ceraso
EUGENE .... Johnny Giacalone
MILTON .... William Wise/James DeMarse
REENA .... Amy Staats

CHARACTERS

LUCIA — thirty-five, an artist.

JULIET — her mother. She is a kind of ghost; she appears
in the play as a woman about Lucia's age, looking healthy
but somewhat ethereal.

JEREMY — Lucia's ex-husband.

EUGENE — twenty-five, a med student.

MILTON — Eugene's father.

REENA — another med student.

PLACE

Coney Island, New York.

TIME

Present.

NOTE ON THE SET: The set must be able to convey various
locations. The two most important elements which should remain
onstage throughout the play are 1) a large canvas on which Lucia
builds her mosaic throughout the play and 2) something sugges-
tive of Coney Island — for example, a piece of the Cyclone or the
Wonder Wheel.

NOTE ON TRANSITIONS: Scenes do not need to end in black-
out. Transitions between scenes can be fluid and can include subtle
interaction between characters. Characters can carry set pieces on
and off themselves.

SUMMER CYCLONE

ACT ONE

Scene 1

Coney Island. Carnival music. Lucia enters, collecting seashells. Juliet enters, holding a small carousel horse figurine.

JULIET. Four reasons to like Coney Island. Number four.
LUCIA. I used to come here every year, when I was a kid.
JULIET. Because I brought you —
LUCIA. Yeah, in November, when everything was closed.
JULIET. You hated it.
LUCIA. Did I?
JULIET. Number three.
LUCIA. There used to be a ride called the Shangrila-Ha-Ha. I mean it doesn't get much better than that.
JULIET. Number two.
LUCIA. People come here wanting things to spin out of control. They actually want that, to get flipped upside down, and to get nauseous. They eat hot dogs and cotton candy and they go on the Tilt a' Whirl and they want to be nauseous.
JULIET. Sounds lovely.
LUCIA. Might be nice. If I get sick of being nauseous all by myself.
JULIET. And number one.
LUCIA. Anything can happen. It's that kind of place. I mean Shangrila-Ha-Ha. Anything could —
JULIET. Do you believe that?
LUCIA. Sometimes.
JULIET. *(Holding out her carousel horse.)* Did you ride the carousel?
LUCIA. Not today. What's that for?

JULIET. It's a wedding present.
LUCIA. For who? ... You only get a year. Then it's too late. Everybody knows that.
JULIET. Well. I was in France.
LUCIA. I realize that.
JULIET. A small town, near Paris.
LUCIA. What was it called?
JULIET. Can't remember. But it was pretty. C'étais jolie —
LUCIA. I don't know French.
JULIET. You should get one of those phrase books, in case you decide to go.
LUCIA. I'm not going to France.
JULIET. What are those?
LUCIA. Seashells. And broken glass.
JULIET. You could make a mosaic.
LUCIA. Yeah, well, that's what I do. Make mosaics. So I will.
JULIET. What kind.
LUCIA. I don't know yet.
JULIET. Anything could happen?
LUCIA. Yes.
JULIET. Good luck. *(Juliet exits.)*

Scene 2

The hospital. Eugene enters, wearing a white coat. He sits on the edge of a desk and looks over some papers. He begins practicing what he would say if he were the doctor, trying out different official-sounding voices.

EUGENE. It's important that you realize, that a clinical trial ... *(He clears his throat. Lucia enters and crosses towards Eugene, but he does not see her.)* It's always important, to realize, that a clinical trial, has certain ... *(Trying again.)* It's important ... I feel that I should warn you ...

LUCIA. Excuse me ...

EUGENE. Hi — sorry — *(Eugene gets up, knocking over a mug filled with pencils.)*

LUCIA. Sorry, I was looking for Dr. Slogan's office?

EUGENE. *(Gathering the pencils.)* Yes. Hi. Can I help you with something?

LUCIA. You're ... Dr. Slogan?

EUGENE. No — sorry. I'm working with him. But this is his office.

LUCIA. I just wanted to find out if I would have a chance to meet with Dr. Slogan this morning.

EUGENE. Is he expecting you? His schedule is pretty tight this morning ... he's getting a clinical trial set up, meeting with patients ...

LUCIA. Yes. That's what I'm talking about, the clinical trial. There was a lot of paperwork out there, but I was hoping to ask Dr. Slogan some questions.

EUGENE. Right, okay ... what's the patient's name?

LUCIA. My name? Lucia Pollner.

EUGENE. No, the — right. Sorry — Lucia Pollner, did you say.

LUCIA. Yeah. You know people don't look like patients. They are patients.

EUGENE. I know that. I'm sorry.

LUCIA. I mean you don't necessarily look like a doctor.

EUGENE. Well I'm not. Yet. I'm in medical school. My name's Eugene Dillon. *(He goes to shake her hand and knocks over the pencils again.)*

LUCIA. Is this your first day?

EUGENE. Yes. Yes it is.

LUCIA. They're rough ... first days.

EUGENE. Look, I'm sorry, about all this. Dr. Slogan does want to meet with everyone today. He's just a little delayed. But I'm sure he will start calling people in soon.

LUCIA. Okay. Thanks.

EUGENE. I'll let him know you're waiting.

LUCIA. Thank you. *(Lucia exits. Milton enters.)*

MILTON. You feel sometimes as if you're swimming in a soup, some kind of soup, a minestrone. And these things float by, a bean, or a noodle, or a carrot. And you think, these things you recognize, you can identify. You understand this soup, you are in control. But maybe there are other things, floating by, and you're not sure, they are ambiguous. Maybe it feels sometimes like you will lose yourself, be overwhelmed, by the soup.

EUGENE. Dad.

MILTON. Yes.

EUGENE. What are you talking about?

MILTON. Medicine. I am talking about the practice of medicine. You are about to embark on this journey, and you will come out a doctor at the other end. And the school is good, we know the school is good, but I want you to understand it is not easy. It is never easy. You are always, no matter which school, no matter how many years, in the soup. *(Loud rock music begins. Reena enters, dancing to the music, her back to the audience.)* Good luck. Study hard.

EUGENE. Okay. *(Milton exits. Eugene crosses to Reena. They speak loudly, over the music.)* HEY.

REENA. *(Still dancing.)* HEY. HOW'S IT GOING.

EUGENE. OKAY. I WAS WONDERING IF YOU'D BE HERE.

REENA. WHAT?

EUGENE. I WAS WONDERING, BECAUSE THE OTHER NIGHT —

REENA. WHAT?

EUGENE. COULD WE … GO … *(Eugene gestures and they move to another part of the stage. The music fades to the background.)*

REENA. Jesus. It's hot in there. *(She lights a cigarette and holds one out to Eugene.)*

EUGENE. No thanks. I quit, just a couple weeks ago.

REENA. Me too. I quit every August. Jesus, long fucking day. Did you start your rotation?

EUGENE. Yeah, chemotherapy trial.

REENA. I was on that, but they just switched everything around. Now it's ear nose throat. They had this woman in today, they stuck a tube down her nose to look at her vocal cords.

EUGENE. That should be interesting.

REENA. The trial sounded better.

EUGENE. Yeah, well, it should be good. Well anyway, I just … wanted to say hi.

REENA. Hi.

EUGENE. Yeah, hi. I didn't get your um phone number or any-
thing, the other night.
REENA. You didn't ask.
EUGENE. Yeah, well I … neither did you …
REENA. I had a good time.
EUGENE. Yeah, me too … would you want to get a drink some
time …
REENA. Yeah, sure.
EUGENE. Okay.
REENA. Cool.
EUGENE. Could I … actually …
REENA. Sure. *(She hands him a cigarette and lights it as they exit.)*

Scene 3

*Lucia's apartment. Lucia is working on her mosaic. Jeremy is
watching, but also flipping through a phrase book.*

LUCIA. What's weird about your phrase book, is it doesn't have
the phrase for I'm sick, which seems stupid, because tourists get
sick, right, they might have to go to the hospital, and it would
make sense if they could explain it to somebody, don't you think.
JEREMY. Je suis malade. I'm sick. It's je suis —
LUCIA. Thank you. I can't believe you're actually here.
JEREMY. Heard my girl was in trouble.
LUCIA. Not a girl. And not yours.
JEREMY. I thought you might need somebody.
LUCIA. To take care of me?
JEREMY. For some support.
LUCIA. I take pretty good care of myself.
JEREMY. Do you believe in ghosts?
LUCIA. No.
JEREMY. Would you believe it if I said your mother sent me?
LUCIA. Please don't say things like that.

JEREMY. I keep having these dreams about her. Since you called the other week, she keeps showing up every night. And it's like somebody's saying, here it is, another chance.
LUCIA. For what? What are you talking about?
JEREMY. To deal with this thing. To do it right, like none of us did before. Because we didn't help her.
LUCIA. She didn't let us. Two doctors, two fucking opinions and she runs off to some little town in France. And why not, if you're going to give up, France is good a place as any.
JEREMY. She was trying to protect you.
LUCIA. I was twenty-four. She sent me lists, not even real letters, just those fucking lists. Five things you should do in New York in April. Ten reasons to marry Jeremy. Five reasons not to postpone the wedding and one reason I won't be there.
JEREMY. Because I'm too sick.
LUCIA. Why are we talking about this.
JEREMY. Because it can be different this time. The doctors know so much more now. You can stay and fight.
LUCIA. I plan to. Believe me, I don't want to make my mom's mistakes, I'd rather make my own.
JEREMY. Okay so that's why I'm here, to see how I can help. What happens next? *(Lucia continues working on the mosaic as she answers, distracting herself from what she is saying.)*
LUCIA. They do the mastectomy … and that's also when they see if it's spread to the lymph nodes, and how many of those. And then I start this chemotherapy drug trial.
JEREMY. With these new drugs, which are more powerful.
LUCIA. Or more toxic. They don't know. The standard treatment doesn't always work so well, so they're hoping this new combination will be better. But I might not get the new drugs. Half of everybody gets the standard stuff.
JEREMY. And how long does this go on for? I want to work out my schedule so I'm available.
LUCIA. Come on, you can't drop everything, you've got your whole exciting life to attend to. You're opening a gallery in Paris. On some Rue. The Rue de something.
JEREMY. The Rue de St. Germain.
LUCIA. Say that again.

JEREMY. The Rue de St. Germain.

LUCIA. Yes. Exactly.

JEREMY. The gallery's tiny. Like a kind of art closet.

LUCIA. Still, I know you don't have time to run back and forth to New York.

JEREMY. I can make time. I have meetings in Philadelphia, I'll figure it out. I can't just stay in Paris, thinking about everything. Ever since your phone call, I wake up with this feeling that I should be doing something ...

LUCIA. There's worse things to wake up with.

JEREMY. Just tell me what you need.

LUCIA. I don't know. It's nice you're here. For tonight anyhow. It's nice ... I have some champagne. So we could do this thing I was reading about today, in the waiting room. Some people do this ceremony, before the surgery, to say goodbye. They toast it.

JEREMY. Toast ... the ...

LUCIA. Breast. Some couples. As a kind of ritual. People do it with their husband. But hey, why not your ex-husband. At least you have some experience, you already did it once.

JEREMY. Did what?

LUCIA. Said goodbye, to my breast.

JEREMY. I don't seem to remember that.

LUCIA. I mean you never saw it again did you.

JEREMY. No, I didn't.

LUCIA. Right. So there you go. *(Lucia hands him a glass of champagne and takes one herself.)*

JEREMY. *(Raising his glass.)* Okay. To ... your ...

LUCIA. Cheers.

JEREMY. To a fine ... breast ...

LUCIA. L'chaim. *(She throws her glass to the floor, smashing it.)*

JEREMY. Can you use that? For your mosaic?

LUCIA. No. I just felt like it. *(Lucia goes to clean up the glass. She is fighting tears and does not want Jeremy to see her face. He grabs her arm.)*

JEREMY. Hey. It's okay. You can —

LUCIA. Thanks. *(She turns away quickly, going to clean up the glass. Jeremy exits as Juliet enters, carrying the carousel horse.)*

JULIET. The thing about Paris is, once you start thinking about

it you can't stop. One hundred things to love about Paris. Number one hundred, the cafés. Ninety-nine, crepes. Ninety-eight, old men with little dogs …
LUCIA. Ten reasons you shouldn't have gone.
JULIET. I'm listening.
LUCIA. You had no business going. You should have stayed, like I'm doing. Gone to the doctor.
JULIET. I did.
LUCIA. Gone to a better one. We would have helped you. You had no business going.
JULIET. How do you say I'm sorry.
LUCIA. I don't know. You just do.
JULIET. Look it up. *(Lucia looks through the phrase book.)* I thought that phrase book would be useful.
LUCIA. Here it is. Je suis désolée.
JULIET. My French was never very good. Even when I lived there. *(Juliet exits.)*

Scene 4

The hospital. Eugene enters with a mass of paperwork, which he begins sorting through. Lucia enters and crosses to him. She is also carrying some papers.

LUCIA. Hi, Eugene, right. I wanted to ask you about this form here.
EUGENE. *(Distracted by his paperwork.)* That's informed consent. It explains the benefits and risks involved in the trial. We just need everybody's signature.
LUCIA. Is Dr. Slogan available? If we have questions.
EUGENE. He was delayed actually. He'll be here tomorrow morning.
LUCIA. Oh — okay. Just one other thing, on this enrollment profile, you've got the wrong occupation listed.
EUGENE. Oh. That's really just for our records.

LUCIA. Okay, but, it says I'm a dentist. I'm an artist. I'm not sure how that happened exactly. I'm not a dentist.
EUGENE. *(Writing something down.)* Okay, I'll make a note of that.
LUCIA. Thanks. And there's one other thing ... my mother's name was Juliet. Not Julia.
EUGENE. Oh, okay, thanks.
LUCIA. Could you change that?
EUGENE. Will do.
LUCIA. You didn't write it down. It's Juliet.
EUGENE. Okay. *(Writing it down.)* ... Just bring that form over when you're ready. *(He turns back to his paperwork.)*
LUCIA. Okay. *(Lucia takes the form and goes to fill it out. Milton enters and crosses to Eugene.)*
MILTON. Aah, there you are. Hard at work.
EUGENE. Hey Dad, what are you doing down here?
MILTON. I had a few minutes between patients. Thought I would come downstairs and say hello. But I don't want to interrupt.
EUGENE. I'm just a little stressful. Dr. Slogan was supposed to be here this afternoon, but he's not and I've got to deal with this paperwork and all these questions.
MILTON. For the clinical trial. We're talking noodles, we're talking leeks, it's like a crock pot full of stew, all this stuff floating in the murk, and you've got to sort it out.
EUGENE. This one's pretty straightforward.
MILTON. Straightforward, hmmn? For you maybe, try asking the patient. Don't tell me you're forgetting about the patient.
EUGENE. Look, I'm not —
MILTON. You think it's an easy decision, for a patient to participate in one of these things? You think it's easy, to agree to some unknown course of action with who knows what results.
EUGENE. Look, I don't forget about the patient. But you can't think like that all the time. I can't.
MILTON. You have to. You have to remember that this is somebody's life you're dealing with, it's not just numbers, and science.
EUGENE. I can't do that — it messes me up. Because then I start thinking about Mom — and then I can't think straight. Doesn't that happen to you?
MILTON. Of course that happens to me.

EUGENE. Well it messes everything up. And I have to think straight. So stop saying things like that, okay?
MILTON. Here, take a look at this clipping. You see that picture, this woman decided not to get breast reconstruction. Instead she got this tattoo of a bird, right there. You see that, that's called courage. So take a look at that picture, next time you find yourself forgetting about the patient.
EUGENE. Dad, I just asked you —
MILTON. And I'm asking you to stop thinking so straight. Take a good look at that picture. *(Lucia approaches.)*
EUGENE. Okay, fine, thanks.
MILTON. Well I'll leave you to it. Good luck. *(Milton exits. Eugene turns back to his paperwork.)*
LUCIA. Hi, I should probably ask Dr. Slogan this, but I'm wondering, this paragraph where it talks about the new drugs possibly having harmful side effects ...
EUGENE. Well, that's highly unlikely.
LUCIA. What is.
EUGENE. The side effects will be closely monitored. Any sign of harm, and we would suspend the treatment.
LUCIA. Okay, right. And also, if they found out that the new treatment was really working for people, would people with the older treatment get switched to the new one?
EUGENE. No. Not in the course of the study.
LUCIA. Okay. Could I actually get another copy of that form, I wrote questions all over mine.
EUGENE. Sure. One second. *(Eugene tries to find the form in everything he is carrying and accidentally drops several papers, including the clipping.)*
LUCIA. You only get one first day.
EUGENE. Yeah ... *(She goes to help him pick up the papers.)*
LUCIA. Oh, you've got it — that tattoo picture — the bird. I just did it. Not the real thing, my own version. Symbolic. *(Lucia shows Eugene a tattoo on her shoulder blade.)* Baby bird. For solidarity.
EUGENE. Yeah, that's um ... it's ...
LUCIA. ... I guess I didn't really need to show you that. Could I get that form?
EUGENE. *(Handing her the form.)* Yeah. Here you go.

LUCIA. Okay. *(She turns to go.)*
EUGENE. Ms. Pollner? ... Thanks.
LUCIA. For what?
EUGENE. The tattoo, it's ... I don't know, inspiring.
LUCIA. Yeah? Anytime. *(She turns again and crosses the stage, reading the form.)*
EUGENE. Um wait — Ms. Pollner —
LUCIA. Please, Lucia.
EUGENE. Okay — I just wanted to say, you're right to read that so carefully. Because these trials, they're not always easy.
LUCIA. I don't expect it to be easy.
EUGENE. Yeah, I just wanted to say ... these things do get complicated, there are all kinds of issues, like a, like there's this crock pot —
LUCIA. A crock pot.
EUGENE. No, I didn't mean that, what I meant was, I was talking to my father, he's got this thing, he talks about this soup thing ... with like noodles ...
LUCIA. Crock pot or crackpot.
EUGENE. No — wait I — I just think it's good, you're asking questions. It's a big decision.
LUCIA. Yeah, except it's one of those sort of non-decision decisions. When you don't really have so many options.
EUGENE. You can come back tomorrow, if you want, and ask Dr. Slogan your questions. We don't need that form today.
LUCIA. Are you sure? My surgery is Monday.
EUGENE. It should be fine. I think it's important that you feel right about this.
LUCIA. Thank you.

Scene 5

The hospital. Lucia is in surgery. Juliet enters.

JULIET. Sweet dreams. Sweet sweet dreams. Do you think people dream in surgery. Do you think somebody is cutting into you with a knife, and you're lost somewhere in soft pillows. I dream sometimes … there's this baby crying, and I find her all wrapped up in blankets and I take her in my arms. And maybe a child has a memory of her mother's breast, and maybe she remembers? This is where I went, for milk, for strength, when I was so hungry … There's this baby crying and I know she's hungry because she's grabbing at me with her little grabbing fingers. So I unbutton my shirt one button, two, three … and there it is, under my shirt just like always. Because you have to be ready when there's a baby grabbing at you. I have this dream sometimes, there's a baby crying. But it's not my baby. My baby is thirty-five. She doesn't drink milk. But maybe she remembers? Grabbing at me with little grabbing fingers. Maybe she remembers. Where to go, when she's hungry. *(Juliet exits. Eugene enters. He places a rolled-up print near the bed and exits. Lucia sits up slowly, addressing Jeremy, but not speaking to him directly.)*
LUCIA. You wake up, but you keep your eyes closed, just in case you're wrong, just in case the life you're about to wake up in is not the right one at all, just in case you can still somehow switch it. Jeremy, you know how sometimes … *(Jeremy enters. They are not speaking directly to each other.)*
JEREMY. You keep your eyes closed, as if somehow this person will materialize next to you. Because you can feel it, with your whole body, the empty space next to you in the bed, but you think maybe if I keep my eyes closed, then when I open them, maybe …
LUCIA. You wake up and you have these tubes hanging out of you, and you think I wonder how a soldier feels when he wakes up after a battle and says I have to check if I have two legs and two

16

arms and two of everything.

JEREMY. You wake up and you're alone. And the place feels so strange.

LUCIA. This nurse is standing there, and she's holding this Picasso print and she says see there's this picture, somebody left this for you and you ask did it spread … and she says I have to change the dressing, I'll teach you how later and you say how many. And she says the doctor will be by soon to tell you about the lymph nodes and you say how many and she says, and you say how many and she says nine.

JEREMY. You wake up.

LUCIA. The place feels so strange.

JEREMY. You wish sometimes you could keep your eyes closed …

LUCIA. I want to go back to sleep …

JEREMY. And maybe you'll wake up somewhere else entirely. *(Jeremy exits.)*

Scene 6

A coffee shop. Lucia and Eugene enter.

LUCIA. Hi. Eugene. They said over at the hospital I could find you here.

EUGENE. With my fellow refugees.

LUCIA. Refugees?

EUGENE. All these people. Fleeing, the hospital cafeteria.

LUCIA. Yeah, well, those are pretty horrible places.

EUGENE. Depressing.

LUCIA. I just wanted to thank you, for the Picasso print.

EUGENE. Oh, yeah, you got it okay? I just wanted you to know that I know that you're not a dentist. But I don't even know if you like Picasso.

LUCIA. No, I do. You know, depending on the angle you look at it, it's interesting how the woman has either one breast or seven …

EUGENE. Oh — I wasn't — I mean I didn't —

LUCIA. Kidding. Kidding. It was a very nice thing, to get, out of the blue.

EUGENE. Good.

LUCIA. So, here we are. Are you busy with Dr. Slogan, preparing for the trial?

EUGENE. There's a lot of organizational work. Setting up the files, and assigning codes, to set up the blind.

LUCIA. So we don't know which drugs we're getting.

EUGENE. Yeah.

LUCIA. Will you know?

EUGENE. Not me personally. It's a single blind trial, so Dr. Slogan will, but they're being pretty strict about who sees the information, and I'm pretty low on the pole, as they say. When is your first treatment?

LUCIA. A week from Wednesday.

EUGENE. Are you going somewhere, or treating yourself to something before chemo starts?

LUCIA. Not really. I've been pretty much operating from hour to hour. But that's not a bad idea. To go someplace to be crazy, normal …

EUGENE. Where would you want to go?

LUCIA. I don't know … Wait, I do know, Coney Island. I'm thinking if I ate all kinds of shit and went on the Cyclone maybe later I could trick my body into thinking that when I get nauseous, it's because I'm having fun.

EUGENE. That sounds like a plan.

LUCIA. It does, doesn't it? Coney Island.

EUGENE. Why not.

LUCIA. Why the fuck not. I'll have to drag somebody.

EUGENE. Who would turn down a trip to Coney Island?

LUCIA. Have you been there?

EUGENE. No.

LUCIA. You'd be surprised. Some people find it creepy, or something. Well, anyway, Eugene, thank you again, for the print.

EUGENE. Sure. I guess I'll see you at the hospital next week then.

LUCIA. Yeah, I guess so.

EUGENE. I'm glad you came by.

LUCIA. Yeah, okay. I'll see you later.

EUGENE. Okay. I'll see you. *(Lucia exits. Eugene begins to read his book. Lucia enters again, crosses to him.)*

LUCIA. Look, do you want to go?

EUGENE. Do I —

LUCIA. Yeah, Coney Island. On Saturday. Would you go with me?

EUGENE. I — I'm sorry, I really can't —

LUCIA. I'm sorry. That was stupid. I shouldn't have … forget it. *(Lucia begins backing away.)*

EUGENE. I could go on Sunday.

LUCIA. You could?

EUGENE. Yeah, sure.

LUCIA. Okay. Are you sure it's — this is — We'll go Sunday. Okay.

EUGENE. Okay.

LUCIA. All right.

EUGENE. Should I get your number.

LUCIA. Yeah, okay. *(She scribbles her number on a napkin.)*

EUGENE. So I'll call you. I should get back.

LUCIA. Okay. I'll talk to you later then. *(Lucia exits.)*

Scene 7

Lucia's apartment. Lucia enters and begins working on her mosaic. Jeremy enters with a picnic basket.

JEREMY. How's it coming?

LUCIA. Pretty good. I still haven't figured out what it is I'm making.

JEREMY. Are you ready? Because we are having a day. A very busy day of things.

LUCIA. We are?

JEREMY. I'm working them out. The brain is working on it. My

Philadelphia meetings got pushed back to tomorrow, so we're all set. I mean Central Park, for example, I'm talking a good fucking day.

LUCIA. The thing is, Jeremy, you can't just do that.

JEREMY. Do what?

LUCIA. Just blaze into town because you got the day off, no warning.

JEREMY. I called.

LUCIA. Yeah, you left a message last night. I mean I'm glad, I'm glad you're here but you can't expect that I'm totally free, I mean my life's not at a total standstill.

JEREMY. What are you saying?

LUCIA. I'm saying I have plans. I'm supposed to go to Coney Island.

JEREMY. I love Coney Island.

LUCIA. I'm meeting somebody.

JEREMY. Oh. Right.

LUCIA. I'm sorry, it was the same idea that you had, to do something while I'm feeling good. And I didn't know you were coming.

JEREMY. Who are you meeting?

LUCIA. This guy, it's kind of random. This kid, he's in med school, he's helping with the study at the hospital. He's part of this whole team.

JEREMY. He's like your doctor?

LUCIA. No.

JEREMY. I fly in from Paris, and it turns out you're going to Coney Island with your doctor.

LUCIA. Med school. He's nobody's doctor yet.

JEREMY. And what, this is like a date, with nobody's doctor.

LUCIA. It's not a date. And it's not, frankly, your business.

JEREMY. How old is this guy?

LUCIA. I don't know.

JEREMY. But a med student, right, so pretty young.

LUCIA. I don't have to explain this to you.

JEREMY. I mean there must be rules right, if he's working on this study and all, I mean this can't be the way things are done.

LUCIA. Since when do you care about the way things are done.

JEREMY. I'm just saying —

LUCIA. You're just pissed off. Because you had this whole day planned, which I appreciate, but it just happens, that I had a ... different day planned.

JEREMY. Apparently.

LUCIA. What is your problem, you still think you can just waltz in and start arranging everybody's everything for them. I can make my own arrangements now, thank you very much. And are you ... I'm sorry, but is it possible that you are ... jealous?

JEREMY. Look, I don't know, I just — find these days ... I'm thinking about you all the time.

LUCIA. Yeah, well, that's called pity. And I don't want it.

JEREMY. It's called I miss you.

LUCIA. You don't just start missing somebody. After all this time, you don't just one day find yourself ...

JEREMY. What, so you never feel that way?

LUCIA. Of course I miss you. But I've been missing you for four years. It's part of my routine, I get up in the morning and I brush my teeth and I miss you. And then I eat breakfast.

JEREMY. So what are you saying.

LUCIA. I don't know, what are you saying?

JEREMY. That we should spend the day together.

LUCIA. I'd like to. Some other day.

JEREMY. Yeah, maybe next time. *(Jeremy exits.)*

Scene 8

Coney Island. Carnival music. Eugene and Lucia enter. Eugene is carrying an orange stuffed octopus.

EUGENE. I mean you saw that, right, how many I got.

LUCIA. Which time are you talking about?

EUGENE. What do you mean which time, the last time.

LUCIA. The fifth time.

EUGENE. Yes the fifth time, the time I won.

LUCIA. I would have to say many. It seemed like many prairie dogs were … gotten.

EUGENE. Right, many. I think it's groundhogs, I'm not sure but I think. Anyway, many. I got nearly all of them.

LUCIA. It was … impressive.

EUGENE. And it was the right choice, wasn't it, the octopus, because that other thing, that purple thing …

LUCIA. It was like a sloth.

EUGENE. Yeah, it was, like some kind of sloth. And who needs that, right, a purple sloth thing. I mean definitely the octopus.

LUCIA. No question.

EUGENE. You think it's ridiculous, right, you think I'm … young.

LUCIA. You are young.

EUGENE. It's not that big a difference.

LUCIA. How would you know?

EUGENE. I interviewed you.

LUCIA. That's right, you did. Well that takes some of the fun out of small talk, doesn't it.

EUGENE. I'm sorry, we promised we wouldn't mention the study.

LUCIA. Yeah, we did. So how old are you?

EUGENE. Twenty-five.

LUCIA. Almost legal.

EUGENE. For what?

LUCIA. Insight.

EUGENE. That's not exactly fair.

LUCIA. I'm only kidding. I'm sure you understand a great many things.

EUGENE. Some things.

LUCIA. Good. Learn to fake the rest. Good skill for a doctor. You have to explain the world to people.

EUGENE. Not the world …

LUCIA. Sometimes. How did you decide, that you wanted to be a doctor.

EUGENE. I hate that question. No matter what you say, it never sounds right …

LUCIA. You want to help people.

EUGENE. Something like that. It's the power of knowledge. When things are so … cloudy. Because you know things, so you can … right, help.

LUCIA. It sounds all right.

EUGENE. My first day of medical school they told us to buy those clicky pens, those pens that change color when you click. They said it would help, to use those for notes, and diagrams. Now it's all you hear, in class, click click click. Sometimes I wonder if anybody's thinking about anything other than switching colors. Click red, click blue. Like kindergarten.

LUCIA. Can't be like that all the time. Cutting up bodies, right, that's not kindergarten.

EUGENE. No.

LUCIA. More like seventh grade, frogs and Styrofoam.

EUGENE. It's pretty different.

LUCIA. I'm sure it is. But look at you, you do look like some kid, you're toting an octopus for God's sake.

EUGENE. I'm not the one who suggested an amusement park.

LUCIA. Fair enough.

EUGENE. And I want that on record, if there's trouble.

LUCIA. You expecting some kind of trouble?

EUGENE. I'm not expecting anything. *(They look at each other, the moment suddenly feels awkward.)* … You know I didn't say anything about this, to Dr. Slogan.

LUCIA. I didn't think you would have.

EUGENE. I mean it's none of his business, is it, where you or I goes on a Sunday afternoon.

LUCIA. This place is unlike any place in the world. My mom used to take me in the winter, when it was all eerie and deserted.

EUGENE. Yeah, why winter?

LUCIA. I don't know. But I used to get scared, too many ghosts and weirdos running around.

EUGENE. Ghosts?

LUCIA. You know when my mother died, she was cremated and I came here with the ashes to, what's the word, spread … scatter … release? I can never think of the word.

EUGENE. You did it here?

LUCIA. Yeah, she died in France, and I wasn't there.

EUGENE. My mom died too, when I was sixteen.

LUCIA. Oh — I'm sorry.

EUGENE. Yeah, well, you know …

LUCIA. Yeah. Would you … want to get some hot dogs? My kitchen at home is full of vegetables and brown rice and extra-firm tofu and I think we should get some hot dogs.
EUGENE. Is it all right?
LUCIA. I don't know doctor, you tell me.
EUGENE. Sorry, I — hot dogs it is. You like sauerkraut?
LUCIA. Love it.
EUGENE. Just one thing. Take this. *(He holds out the octopus.)*
LUCIA. Oh no you don't.
EUGENE. Take it.
LUCIA. I'm not. I'm sorry.
EUGENE. Take the octopus.
LUCIA. I don't want it.
EUGENE. Neither do I.
LUCIA. You won it. You tried five times.
EUGENE. I was proving myself.
LUCIA. Your ability to conk prairie dogs on the head.
EUGENE. It's groundhogs I'm pretty sure. And I need a backup career.
LUCIA. Yeah, I'm beginning to think you do.
EUGENE. What I don't need, is an octopus. *(Eugene pushes the octopus in Lucia's direction. They struggle over it.)*
LUCIA. Fine, I'm taking it and just watch, I'm going to throw in the ocean and something will chew on it and die.
EUGENE. Nothing will touch it. It's the color of macaroni and cheese.
LUCIA. Come on — last chance to save some poor sea creature. *(She waits to see what Eugene will do. He looks as if he is letting her keep it and then suddenly changes his mind and rushes for it. They struggle some more and find themselves very close together. An awkward moment which could turn into a kiss but doesn't quite. Eugene breaks the moment, turning or stepping back.)*
EUGENE. I think it's about that time.
LUCIA. What time is that?
EUGENE. Cyclone time. What do you say, roller coaster?
LUCIA. I think I'm already on one.
EUGENE. Let's try that again. Roller coaster?
LUCIA. Yes. Fuck yes. *(Eugene leads the way. He exits as Juliet*

enters, stopping Lucia from exiting. Juliet carries the carousel horse.)
JULIET. Six reasons not to go to Coney Island with your doctor.
LUCIA. GO AWAY.
JULIET. Number six. We hate doctors.
LUCIA. He's not my doctor. Why are you always carrying that thing?
JULIET. I told you, it's a wedding present.
LUCIA. I don't want it.
JULIET. I'm keeping it safe so nothing happens to it. Number five, the doctor won't let you eat hot dogs.
LUCIA. He bought me hot dogs. Three, if you must know.
JULIET. Number four, you yourself are always saying, the thing about Coney Island, anything can happen.
LUCIA. So?
JULIET. Which means number three there might be a compromising situation, number two you might lose yourself, number one you might have a good time.
LUCIA. I did. A very good time.
JULIET. I'm saying be careful.
LUCIA. Why?
JULIET. Because it hurts. You let yourself feel things and you eat hot dogs and you walk in the sand and you laugh at somebody and you feel things and it hurts. You have no idea. I am trying to protect you.
LUCIA. I don't want your protection. I never wanted it.
JULIET. Did I ever tell you why I like Coney Island in the winter?
LUCIA. No, but I bet I can guess. It's all shut down, is that it?
JULIET. You have no idea.
LUCIA. Yes I do. I've seen it like that, you know I have. All these rides, all silent and locked into place. So you couldn't ride them even if you wanted to, no risks, no thrills. Just painted skeletons of a place that had some sliver of a life last season and a real life, something loud and rich, years and years back. But today was different. No skeletons. Kids and fat moms and music and everything else. And I went on the oldest standing roller coaster in the universe, and you can't take that away so don't you even try.
JULIET. Are you done?
LUCIA. Yeah, for now.

JULIET. Me too.
LUCIA.   Good, because I'm going home. I have actually an appointment in the morning.
JULIET. The drugs?
LUCIA. Yes.
JULIET. Are you scared?
LUCIA. I have to be there at eight.
JULIET. That's not what I asked.
LUCIA. So I should go to bed.
JULIET. Good luck. I'll keep my fingers crossed.
LUCIA. Well that's a comfort.
JULIET. Never mind then.
LUCIA. Wait — would you — please.
JULIET. Goodnight baby.

Scene 9

The coffee shop. Eugene is at a table, studying. Milton enters.

MILTON. I thought I might find you here. Hitting the books. Memorizing your facts.
EUGENE. Hi Dad.
MILTON. Time to take a break.
EUGENE. I can't really. I'm stressed out.
MILTON. We have an important errand. Have I told you about my new project? My new passion, if you will. I think you'll find it interesting. I am commissioning artwork, for the hospital. I have been reading about the healing powers of art. Not just the creation of art, but the viewing of it. What do you think, do you believe that a painting could heal somebody?
EUGENE. I don't know.
MILTON. I'm asking your opinion.
EUGENE. Well it could maybe comfort them.
MILTON. Interesting. Interesting distinction. We shall see. I'm

working with a fascinating artist, his name is Rudolph Rudolph.
EUGENE. Rudolph Rudolph?
MILTON. He believes that art can inspire healing. And he's going to do a series of canvases for us.
EUGENE. Sounds great.
MILTON. I am on my way, to the studio of Mr. Rudolph. In SoHo. And I thought you might want to accompany me.
EUGENE. Right now? Sorry, I can't.
MILTON. This is not something you're going to find in your curriculum. I tell you, healing is a great mystery. And our part of that mystery is so narrow. Come with me, it will open your eyes.
EUGENE. I really can't — I told you, I'm totally stressed out. I have a big exam tomorrow. I have to study, I was out all day.
MILTON. Yes, I left you a message.
EUGENE. I was at Coney Island.
MILTON. Were you. What were you doing?
EUGENE. I don't know. Exploring. I'm not sure how I managed never to go there before.
MILTON. Didn't we ever bring you there, when you were a kid. I'm sure we meant to. You know your mother and I went to Coney Island on one of our first dates. Did I ever tell you that? We rode the Shangrila-Ha-Ha.
EUGENE. The what?
MILTON. Can you believe it? She loved it. I kept trying to win her one of those stuffed creatures. Some purple nonsense, I can't remember. What an extraordinary place ...
EUGENE. I had fun. But now I'm in trouble.
MILTON. What is your exam on?
EUGENE. Oncology.
MILTON. Well, you should be in good shape for that, from the trial you're working on.
EUGENE. Yeah, it's just, strange to read all this about chemotherapy. How it works, killing all the cells, I mean I've read this stuff before, but now it seems different, I guess because it hits pretty close to what I'm dealing with. At the hospital.
MILTON. Now that is the kind of thing I have been waiting to hear you say. That sounds like the observation of a person who is interested in more than facts. A person who is remembering to

think about the patient.
EUGENE. Yeah, well I guess I am.
MILTON. Congratulations.
EUGENE. I'm not sure it's anything to congratulate. And it's certainly not helping me study.
MILTON. You'll do fine. And you are broadening your perspective, which is the important thing.
EUGENE. I guess.
MILTON. Remember, ours is a narrow path. Another time, you'll have to come with me to meet Mr. Rudolph. You always had a good eye, for artwork.
EUGENE. Sure, some other time.
MILTON. Good luck with the exam.

Scene 10

Lucia's apartment. Juliet enters, carrying a wig which she examines tenderly and then places in a box. She exits as Lucia enters. Lucia's hair is now cut very short and she wears a Yankees hat. Eugene enters.

EUGENE. Hi.
LUCIA. Hi. I thought you said you'd call.
EUGENE. I did, a couple of times. No answer. You started your treatment — are you okay?
LUCIA. Yeah; it's nice of you, to come over. I mean I wish I felt better, we could go out or something.
EUGENE. It's okay. Did you … your hair, did you …
LUCIA. Chopped it off. I mean it's not gone, it's just … short. I thought if it starts to … there won't be such a mess. I did it this morning.
EUGENE. You did it yourself?
LUCIA. Yeah, I'm sure it's awful. I kept my eyes closed the whole time, and as soon as I finished I decided I was a Yankees fan, so

that's convenient.

EUGENE. I bet it looks good.

LUCIA. Go Yankees.

EUGENE. Without the hat. Can I …

LUCIA. I did buy a wig. But it's all wrong. *(She pulls out the wig.)* They tell you to buy three, and it's supposed to be one for what you look like, one for what you think you look like, and one for what you want to look like. So I got this one, but it's kind of like what I want to think that other people wished I looked like, or something. I mean it looks terrible and it's weirding me out, sitting in this box and everything, what do you think, I think I should give it to the octopus.

EUGENE. Yeah?

LUCIA. I mean I hate to say it, but it's really perfect for the sloth. I mean if you could have won the sloth, we might really be in business.

EUGENE. I could have won whichever I wanted, it was a choice.

LUCIA. Oh, yeah, that's right, you rejected the sloth.

EUGENE. So did you. You said it was …

LUCIA. What?

EUGENE. Like a … sloth.

LUCIA. Yeah, well, anyhow, grab the octopus, he's over there. *(Eugene holds out the octopus, Lucia puts the wig on him.)* Yeah, I think it works. I think it … works.

EUGENE. I bet your hair looks good. Have you ever had your hair short?

LUCIA. Once. Once I went to this crazy guy who would only cut women's hair really short, even if you asked for something else. He had this photo album of befores and afters and sometimes he would do it for free if he got excited enough. I think somebody sued him or something.

EUGENE. Because you have big eyes. That's why I think it probably looks good.

LUCIA. Yeah?

EUGENE. Yeah.

LUCIA. Well fuck the Yankees.

EUGENE. What?

LUCIA. I mean nobody is ever telling me things like I have big eyes, so here goes, while I'm confident. *(Lucia takes off the hat and*

faces him.)
EUGENE. You look, actually … beautiful.
LUCIA. *(Softly.)* Don't.
EUGENE. I'm serious. I'm not just saying it. You want to look?
LUCIA. No.
EUGENE. I was right, about your eyes … There's just one bit, right here, it's a little longer, or poofy or something …
LUCIA. Can you fix it? Here. *(She hands him the clippers.)*
EUGENE. I've never done this before.
LUCIA. Lots of things I've never done before. And now I have to do them and they suck, so deal.
EUGENE. Okay. *(He reaches out with the clippers, then hesitates; Lucia grabs his hand, holding it in front of her face for a moment. Eugene looks at her, then leans in and kisses her. When he eventually breaks away he stares at the clippers he is still holding.)*
LUCIA. I guess you're one of those people. Who believes in seizing the moment.
EUGENE. I don't know, I guess. Are you?
LUCIA. Depends on the circumstances …
EUGENE. That's the same as no.
LUCIA. Is it?
EUGENE. Last time I checked.
LUCIA. *(Touching the piece of hair he meant to cut.)* It's still — can you … *(Eugene moves to cut the hair and she grabs his hand again. This time she kisses him. After the kiss, he clips the hair.)*
EUGENE. You look really good. I think you should take a look. *(Lucia goes to the mirror.)*
LUCIA. You know what I think?
EUGENE. It looks good. Admit it.
LUCIA. I think you're crazy. I mean hair aside.
EUGENE. Admit it, you like it.
LUCIA. Hair aside, I don't look good. I'm mean this is not Coney Island. I'm not in my glow. I slept in these clothes all morning, and I look, frankly, like somebody going through hell, frankly.
EUGENE. Fine, that's what you think. You know what I think?
LUCIA. The hair, fine. You like it.
EUGENE. I think you're beautiful. Hell aside.
LUCIA. Difficult thing.

EUGENE. What's that?
LUCIA. To put hell to the side.
EUGENE. Yeah. I'm sure.
LUCIA. But thank you.

Scene 11

*Medical school. Eugene enters and kicks the wall in frustration.
Reena enters, smoking a cigarette.*

REENA. Test scores. Mine weren't so good either.
EUGENE. I just expected something a little better.
REENA. I almost died. I mean my mom will kill me. If I don't
do okay on the next one, I will be in hell.
EUGENE. In a way.
REENA. Serious hell.
EUGENE. Well it's never that serious, is it. It's not — we can't
call it hell, because it's just … school.
REENA. Yeah, you can tell yourself that, if it makes you feel better.
Cigarette?
EUGENE. No, thanks. I'm talking about perspective. I mean it's
school, which is not, I mean it's not life.
REENA. It's my life. And yours.
EUGENE. I guess.
REENA. And my parents' money, which they like to remind me
about. Hey, we never got that drink.
EUGENE. Yeah, I'm sorry about that, I guess things got pretty crazy.
REENA. Yeah, tell me about it. I called you on Sunday, but your
roommate said you were out the whole day, the circus or something.
EUGENE. Coney Island.
REENA. Yeah, what were you doing there?
EUGENE. A friend of mine. She wanted to go, so …
REENA. I can't stand that place, gives me the creeps. It's so dirty,
and weird.

EUGENE. I liked it.
REENA. You are a strange bird, Eugene, which I mean is a good thing. You're different from most of the people I'm hanging out with. Like serious. Which is I guess because you have, what did you call it, perspective.
EUGENE. I don't know, maybe some people just grow up fast.
REENA. Yeah, I guess that's it. So would you want to grab a drink this week?
EUGENE. Yeah, sure, it's just everything is so hectic right now.
REENA. Eugene, can I ask you, was it a date? Coney Island?
EUGENE. No. It was … complicated. It was like … an outing.
REENA. Ooh, like Mary Poppins. Well if you feel like another outing, you've got my number.

Scene 12

The coffee shop. Eugene and Lucia enter.

LUCIA. Hey.
EUGENE. Hey, how are you doing.
LUCIA. Okay.
EUGENE. You feel okay?
LUCIA. Well — no — I keep getting these headaches, pretty bad. Is that normal … I mean, does that happen to people?
EUGENE. I think everybody goes through their own reactions.
LUCIA. Yeah, but did you hear about anyone else, with headaches? Because I never read about it.
EUGENE. It could be a lot of things. I mean it's possible, especially if you have the new drugs, that it's just like a side effect.
LUCIA. But did anyone else in the study, did anybody mention it?
EUGENE. You should … talk to Dr. Slogan, if it's bothering you. Because you could ask him, and he could probably tell you more than I could. And that's probably more …
LUCIA. Appropriate?

EUGENE. I'm not really sure, what's appropriate.
LUCIA. Right. Speaking of, I got your message. Dinner.
EUGENE. Yeah, how about Friday.
LUCIA. It sounds nice. But my question is, I mean how many things.
EUGENE. Sorry?
LUCIA. Are wrong, with this picture. I mean so many things.
EUGENE. It's just dinner. An outing.
LUCIA. A what?
EUGENE. Fine, a date.
LUCIA. Yeah, a date. And that's the thing. I'm pretty sure you don't date somebody at a time like this. You know, this is not the time when you start, dating somebody.
EUGENE. Right.
LUCIA. You know.
EUGENE. When do you, start dating somebody.
LUCIA. When it's simple. When there's clarity, when you feel like you have control, in your life.
EUGENE. Uh-huh.
LUCIA. What?
EUGENE. When was the last time anybody felt like that?
LUCIA. I know, what you're saying, but —
EUGENE. What I'm saying —
LUCIA. And what I'm saying is this is different. This is not the usual bundle of issues. I don't know what's going to happen. I mean survival. I don't even know about that.
EUGENE. Nobody knows. Ever. I could get hit by a bus.
LUCIA. That is not the point. Please tell me that you know that is not the point.
EUGENE. Okay.
LUCIA. Please promise me that you will never, talk to me about buses.
EUGENE. Okay. I'm sorry. All I'm saying is —
LUCIA. I know, I know what you're saying.
EUGENE. You're not letting me say it.
LUCIA. Fine.
EUGENE. Have dinner with me. That's what I'm saying. And maybe it's a date, and maybe it's not. And maybe it's appropriate,

and maybe it's not. And maybe we'll have a good time. Or we won't, and either way, it's just dinner. That's it.
LUCIA. That's it, that's what you're saying?
EUGENE. Yeah, but it's your call. If you'd rather close off and make lists of everything that's wrong with the picture, that's your call.
LUCIA. Who said anything about making lists?
EUGENE. You did.
LUCIA. No, because I never —
EUGENE. You said how many things are wrong, so many things. Like you were going to list them all …
LUCIA. I don't make lists.
EUGENE. Like number one, the study, maybe that's not appropriate. Number two maybe you feel like shit, number three —
LUCIA. No, because other people — my mother — other people make lists. I don't.
EUGENE. It doesn't matter. I'm saying it's your call. Dinner.
LUCIA. You want to have dinner … okay … we'll have dinner.
EUGENE. Yeah?
LUCIA. Yeah.
EUGENE. Okay.
LUCIA. Okay.

Scene 13

Lucia's apartment. Lucia is on the floor, surrounded by seashells. Jeremy enters and goes to her, kissing her hello.

JEREMY. What's all this?
LUCIA. Just trying to figure out which ones to use, for the mosaic.
JEREMY. How are you?
LUCIA. Okay. Hungry.
JEREMY. I've got bananas.
LUCIA. French bananas?
JEREMY. Philadelphia. I've been in Philly all week.

LUCIA. That's why you're here.
JEREMY. I'm here to see how you are.
LUCIA. I have all these cravings. For chocolate milk. And cherry pie.
JEREMY. They have you on some kind of anti-nausea drug, right. Because those foods sound a little … colorful.
LUCIA. *(Taking a banana.)* Yes. Yes they are. You're very smart.
JEREMY. I like the hair. That looks good. I thought you were going to get a wig.
LUCIA. I did, but we decided it wasn't working.
JEREMY. We?
LUCIA. I did. I decided. *(The phone rings.)* I don't feel like talking to anybody. *(The phone continues to ring. The machine picks up.)*
EUGENE. *(O.S.)* Hi, Lucy right, we met the other night at that crazy time, over at Pete's, wow … anyway, the only thing I seem to remember is meeting you, and that you were … stunning. So anyway, my name's Eugene and if you want to have dinner some time this Friday, give me a call.
JEREMY. Okay … what's that about, is that kid crazy?
LUCIA. He's not a kid.
JEREMY. But is he crazy?
LUCIA. It's this game we said we'd try to play. Where we pretend we met some other way and pretend everything is different.
JEREMY. How nice, delusion, sounds healthy.
LUCIA. Yeah, well healthy is kind of a foreign concept right now. Anyhow so far we just leave each other stupid messages. We'll try to play it at dinner and see how far we get.
JEREMY. Think we could play at that game? Pretend we just met?
LUCIA. No.
JEREMY. Stakes too high?
LUCIA. Too much history.
JEREMY. Just makes it more of a challenge.
LUCIA. You know what's funny? I'm reading all this about how you might not feel like a woman. You might feel rejected by your lover or whoever, because first it's the breast and then the hair, so they have to tell you how you're still a woman. But the funny thing is I somehow seem to have two guys hanging around. I mean what is that about, have you got some kind of rescue fantasy?

JEREMY. I don't think you're looking to be rescued.
LUCIA. Oh good, you noticed. So then what is this about?
JEREMY. I told you already, I've been missing you.
LUCIA. And what do you want me to do with that? I mean it's been really nice, seeing you, but you can't just keep showing up here because you feel like it, because it fits your schedule. The thing is, I know you Jeremy, and if you're trying to get me back it's on your terms.
JEREMY. What terms? I don't have any terms. I just want to spend some time with you, to see what happens, to see what's possible.
LUCIA. I can't be thinking about future possibilities. I mean what time is it, two-thirty, I can think ahead to maybe two thirty-six. I can ask myself can you make it till two thirty-six. And then I think yes, I can, and that's the future. Does that make sense?
JEREMY. Yeah, I guess it does.
LUCIA. I'm sorry, I just can't. I mean what's French for who the fuck knows.
JEREMY. Je ne sais the fuck pas.
LUCIA. Right. Okay. Je ne sais the fuck pas. *(Lucia gathers a handful of seashells and throws them in the air. They clatter to the floor.)*

ACT TWO

Scene 1

The coffee shop. Eugene and Milton enter.

MILTON. I'm glad we're doing this. I think this is important.
EUGENE. Sure.
MILTON. It's important that we take the time to do this. Coffee, lunch, half an hour even. That we take the time. Hmmn?
EUGENE. Sure.
MILTON. So, school, the exams, the hospital, the great soup, how's it going?
EUGENE. I'm working on that clinical trial, and I wanted to ask you —
MILTON. Yes, the clinical trial. I knew there was something, some other issues we were meaning to discuss. The clinical trial, did I mention that that one can be a real —
EUGENE. Yeah, you did.
MILTON. Soup. If I may use that metaphor.
EUGENE. You always do. Dad, did you ever hear about anybody getting headaches from chemo?
MILTON. Headaches?
EUGENE. Yeah, I talked to this patient who just starting her treatments, and she's getting these terrible headaches. Isn't that unusual?
MILTON. Yes, that is unusual. It's not a typical reaction.
EUGENE. So if she's got these headaches, how do we know if it's from the cancer, or maybe these new drugs?
MILTON. See, there you go, those are the right questions, the questions you have to start asking.
EUGENE. No, I want to know. I'm asking you, this is not some exercise.
MILTON. What do you mean by that, exercise.

37

EUGENE. Can't you just answer my question? About the side effects? Without turning this into a whole big discussion?
MILTON. You're sounding actually a little hostile, Eugene. I'm curious why that is.
EUGENE. Because you can't just answer a simple question. You know what, never mind, I'll ask Dr. Slogan.
MILTON. You do realize, I'm not an expert on chemotherapy.
EUGENE. Yeah, it's fine. The doctor I'm working with, I should ask him anyway.
MILTON. But I do respect a person who knows how to ask a question. I do celebrate questions.
EUGENE. Fine, bravo.
MILTON. You realize I never asked you where this decision came from, medical school. I never assumed you were following in my footsteps. But I did think it was possible we shared a certain passion, for the challenges, of the profession.
EUGENE. It's just, I can't always ... be discussing everything. Theoretically. Always.
MILTON. Tell me, would it satisfy you, to memorize well, to do well on your exams, to know as they say, your stuff, is that what you want, the thing that makes you want to practice medicine.
EUGENE. No.
MILTON. What is it then?
EUGENE. Power. Of knowledge. These awful things happen to people, diseases and whatever, and I want to help them do something, fight back, take control. I don't want to stand and watch, kicking the wall. I don't want that.
MILTON. You're talking about your mother.
EUGENE. Not necessarily, not entirely ...
MILTON. She was a strong strong woman.
EUGENE. I know that.
MILTON. It was I think two weeks after she was gone, you made this decision. Medical school.
EUGENE. Yes.
MILTON. I remember you, kicking the wall. There were scuff marks, lots of them.
EUGENE. I was pissed off.
MILTON. I started kicking it too, when you were at school,

because I saw the marks on the wall and I thought maybe that makes him feel better. You kicked the wall, and then you said I know, I'll be a doctor, because that's where the power is, the answers. But I was already a doctor, and there were no answers. So I started asking questions, I started celebrating, the questions. Because maybe, who knows but maybe that's where the power is.
EUGENE. I'm sorry.
MILTON. For what?
EUGENE. I don't know.
MILTON. I had brought another clipping. Which I thought might be of interest, pertinent, to what you're doing, the chemotherapy trial. But your plate, it sounds as if your plate is full enough. Time to put, the soup bowl, as it were, aside. Another course.
EUGENE. You do love your metaphor.
MILTON. It's in her honor. She made, your mother, the best minestrone, in the world.
EUGENE. What's it about? The clipping.
MILTON. I understand, your focus, right now, it's on other things.
EUGENE. Pertinent, you said, to the trial.
MILTON. Marijuana. The use of marijuana to alleviate side effects of chemotherapy. Highly controversial. But I understand, what you were saying. Exams, you do have your priorities.
EUGENE. I'd like to read it, actually.
MILTON. I'll save it, why don't I, in case you feel at some point, that you miss these conversations.
EUGENE. Give me the clipping.
MILTON. If you ever want to resume these dialogues.
EUGENE. I want the clipping.
MILTON. Sorry?
EUGENE. Would you give me, the goddamn, clipping.
MILTON. Yes, certainly. If you're interested.
EUGENE. I'm interested. I just said —
MILTON. In that case, certainly. *(He gives it to him.)*
EUGENE. Thank you.
MILTON. It's important I think, that we do this. Meet like this, take the time.
EUGENE. Yeah, thank you.
MILTON. You're welcome.

Scene 2

A restaurant. Eugene and Lucia enter.

EUGENE. Hey, how are you?
LUCIA. All right. How are you?
EUGENE. Fine. How are you feeling.
LUCIA. I am feeling ... *(Initiating their game.)* I am feeling like that was a pretty crazy party, wasn't it.
EUGENE. Yeah.
LUCIA. Pete's, was it?
EUGENE. Yeah, Pete's, that's right.
LUCIA. Crazy Pete.
EUGENE. Like a fox, a mad fox.
LUCIA. Where was that party again?
EUGENE. It was downtown, that big loft, remember, and what happened was you were there, dancing, and I saw you and ...
LUCIA. And?
EUGENE. And I walked over, and I was of course wearing my sharp downtown jacket —
LUCIA. Of course.
EUGENE. Which is what I wear when I'm out with Pete. Anyway, so I walked over to you, and I said, well you remember what I said, things.
LUCIA. What things?
EUGENE. Various things. Such as, such as hi, my name's Gene.
LUCIA. And I said hi, I'm Lucy. What do you do? And you said I study architecture.
EUGENE. Architecture.
LUCIA. Yes, Italian I think.
EUGENE. I didn't say medicine.
LUCIA. Oh no, God no. Definitely architecture. Or something. And I remember mentioning that I'm an actress.
EUGENE. Right, that's right. Italian, right?

LUCIA. An Italian actress?
EUGENE. Who plays, often, Italian roles. Or something.
LUCIA. What?
EUGENE. I don't know. I got thrown off.
LUCIA. Stay with me here.
EUGENE. It's harder than I thought. Okay ... I'm back. Hmmn
... did you see that woman, at the party, who tripped over her
platforms?
LUCIA. Yes, she's my roommate. We call her Nan.
EUGENE. Is that her name?
LUCIA. No. Her name is, Loretta.
EUGENE. Aah. *(Reena enters and crosses to them.)*
REENA. Hey, Eugene.
EUGENE. Reena, hi.
REENA. How's it going? So funny to see you here.
EUGENE. Yeah, what are you doing?
REENA. Dinner, I'm meeting my mom.
EUGENE. Yeah, we're just doing the dinner thing too. This is
Lucia ...
REENA. Hi.
LUCIA. Hi. *(An awkward pause.)*
REENA. You look really familiar, have we —
LUCIA. Yeah, we met once.
EUGENE. You know each other?
REENA. Yeah, at the, it was at the ...
LUCIA. That party the other week.
REENA. Oh, I don't know, I thought it was, wasn't it ...
LUCIA. The hospital.
REENA. Right.
LUCIA. Dr. Slogan's office.
REENA. Yeah. That's right ... When I was working on that,
before they switched us all around. Right. Because I thought you
looked familiar, but I couldn't ...
LUCIA. I cut my hair.
REENA. Right ... right. Well. I hope you two have a good ...
evening ... and everything.
LUCIA. Thanks.
REENA. Oh, Eugene, do you have a cigarette?

EUGENE. No, sorry, I don't really … smoke.
REENA. Right. Okay, yeah, I'm just going to go wait for my mom.
LUCIA. Okay.
REENA. Oh, Eugene, I meant to tell you, there's this masquer-
ade party thing, school sponsored, next week, if you're interested.
EUGENE. Yeah, okay.
REENA. Okay. See you later. *(Reena exits.)*
EUGENE. Jesus Christ.
LUCIA. Well, that was cozy.
EUGENE. I mean Jesus Christ.
LUCIA. You're in school with her.
EUGENE. Yeah, I forgot she was working with Dr. Slogan at the
very beginning. When did you meet?
LUCIA. The first information session.
EUGENE. You know, I wonder if she would have remembered
how you knew each other, if you hadn't said anything.
LUCIA. Oh, come on, she knew. The minute she saw me.
EUGENE. I don't know.
LUCIA. What's the matter, you think she's going to get you into
some kind of trouble?
EUGENE. Not really. I mean I don't think she can. I'm just having
dinner.
LUCIA. Then what's the problem?
EUGENE. There's no problem.
LUCIA. Are you embarrassed?
EUGENE. No.
LUCIA. Because if you're embarrassed, I mean if we're sitting here
and you're —
EUGENE. I'm not embarrassed —
LUCIA. Are you sure?
EUGENE. I don't know what you're talking about, there's noth-
ing to be embarrassed about. Look, you want to go to that party?
LUCIA. What party.
EUGENE. The one she said. Next week.
LUCIA. So you're asking me to go with you to some party, at your
school?
EUGENE. Yeah, why not.
LUCIA. I don't think that's such a good idea.

EUGENE. Why, are you embarrassed?

LUCIA. No. No, I'm not, in fact. In fact, I have the next round of chemo next week, and I don't think I'll be in the mood to party with a bunch of med students. Frankly.

EUGENE. God, I'm sorry.

LUCIA. Don't apologize. Please, don't start, apologizing.

EUGENE. Can we start over? And keep ourselves in, reality.

LUCIA. Sure. Whose reality, yours or mine?

EUGENE. I want to show you something, this clipping, my dad gave it to me. It's on pot, how smoking pot helps you deal with the side effects, during chemo. I thought it might work for your headaches.

LUCIA. Yeah?

EUGENE. So I figured you should read it, and if you want me to get you some, I probably could. Because it's probably easier to find, in my reality.

LUCIA. Probably.

EUGENE. Which is a good thing, about how these things intersect, don't you think.

LUCIA. Yeah, I guess, what are you talking about?

EUGENE. Pot. How you and I should smoke some.

LUCIA. Fascinating …

EUGENE. Because there's doctors in that article, who think it's helpful. And even if they're wrong …

LUCIA. Who gives a shit.

EUGENE. Right, I figured you'd say that. So I'll see what I can do. Okay?

LUCIA. Okay.

Scene 3

Medical school. Reena and Eugene enter.

REENA. So that was interesting …
EUGENE. Hi.
REENA. I thought. I thought what an interesting situation.
EUGENE. There was no situation.
REENA. I thought how interesting that Eugene is out with a patient from the hospital.
EUGENE. Look, it's really my business.
REENA. I thought I wonder if that's a conflict of some kind, ethically speaking.
EUGENE. I think it's not.
REENA. And I thought I wonder how that happened. Which is, you're right, your business.
EUGENE. Yeah. Look, there's nothing I can do, if you're going to say anything …
REENA. Do you like her?
EUGENE. Yeah, I do.
REENA. And that's got to be hard, with everything she's going through. I mean most guys would run the other direction.
EUGENE. I guess.
REENA. You're supposed to say: I'm not most guys. You're supposed to say something like that, heroic.
EUGENE. I'm not trying to be heroic.
REENA. Are you sure?
EUGENE. Yes.
REENA. Okay.
EUGENE. It's not about that.
REENA. Okay.
EUGENE. You have no idea. You don't know the first thing about it.
REENA. The first thing about what.

EUGENE. What it's like. What she's going through.
REENA. And you do.
EUGENE. I'm just trying to be there, to understand how fuck-
ing hard it is.
REENA. Because you think you can make it easier.
EUGENE. I'm not too sure about that.
REENA. Neither am I. Because you could also make it harder,
that's what I think.
EUGENE. Well now I know what you think.
REENA. I wouldn't say anything to anybody, I hope you know that.
EUGENE. Thank you.
REENA. I like you too much, which is the sad thing.
EUGENE. Look, Reena …
REENA. One of them. One of the sad things.

Scene 4

*Lucia's apartment. Lucia enters, and finds Juliet waiting
for her.*

JULIET. Well that was a success.
LUCIA. Oh good, you're back, because I was really starting to
wonder.
JULIET. Crazy Pete's loft party, I mean really.
LUCIA. I was starting to wonder where the doubts go when you
really need them.
JULIET. How do you feel?
LUCIA. I have a killer headache.
JULIET. Ten questions to ask when you're participating in a clinical
trial.
LUCIA. I don't want to hear it.
JULIET. Number ten: Which drug do I get?
LUCIA. That's the whole point, not to know that.
JULIET. Number nine, why do I keep getting headaches? Number

eight, could that be the cancer, number seven, could it be a side effect of the new treatment, number six — or the old treatment? Number five why do I feel like nobody has any answers, number four would it matter if they did, number three am I going to survive this, number two why would anybody want to kiss me right now, number one do I kiss them back?
LUCIA. I don't know. Je ne sais the fuck pas.
JULIET. Is that French?
LUCIA. You tell me.
JULIET. I can't remember.

Scene 5

Lucia's apartment. Eugene enters with a pipe which he shares with Lucia. They are already stoned as the scene begins.

EUGENE. Wait wait wait …
LUCIA. I know. Cranberry juice, I've got some … somewhere. Oh my God, I haven't done this in years. I mean I can't even remember. But it's great, you know, because everything is suddenly so so so …
EUGENE. Wait wait, we were going to get some …
LUCIA. Cranberry juice. Yeah.
EUGENE. Do you want to smoke any more?
LUCIA. I'd better not, right, because we're supposed to save it, for the chemo.
EUGENE. We've got plenty. *(Lucia find the cranberry juice and pours a glass. Eugene hands her the pipe.)*
LUCIA. Oooh, I'm serious, the cranberry juice … there's nothing … I remembered that …
EUGENE. *(Crossing to the mosaic.)* You know this is looking really amazing. I mean it looks like a … I really like it. It's all like …
LUCIA. Thanks.
EUGENE. Yeah. Wait wait, where's the octopus?

LUCIA. The sloth?
EUGENE. Where did you put him?
LUCIA. I'll get him. *(She goes to retrieve the octopus and returns. The octopus is still wearing the wig.)* I think he's very smart. I think he's like a Buddha. Watching everything that goes on. Like we could ask him questions.
EUGENE. What kind of questions?
LUCIA. Like an Oracle. Like I don't know, like why does the cranberry juice taste so good ...
EUGENE. Because we're —
LUCIA. Yeah, yeah yeah. Like does he miss Coney Island?
EUGENE. The octopus?
LUCIA. Because maybe, I mean, was he maybe married to the sloth. I think he's very smart, I think he could answer all kinds of questions. Like what really goes on at Coney Island? Like even I could ask him about my chemo, which drugs I'm getting.
EUGENE. What?
LUCIA. The new drugs or the standard ones. If the octopus could tell me ...
EUGENE. Where did this come ... ?
LUCIA. Or if somebody else could tell me. If you could maybe tell me.
EUGENE. What are you saying ...
LUCIA. Could you find out. Look in the file.
EUGENE. The files are confidential.
LUCIA. Yeah, but if you wanted to ... could you get to them?
EUGENE. No, I can't do that —
LUCIA. Yeah, of course not. Never mind.
EUGENE. Lucia, really, I mean I can't ... it would compromise everything ... the trial, the whole thing. Where did this come from ...
LUCIA. From headaches. From all the ... uncertainty. So you start wanting something certain you could hold on to, information. It's just ... information.
EUGENE. Confidential. Very confidential information.
LUCIA. Yeah, forget it. I just thought maybe you could ...
EUGENE. I really can't. I mean I really ...
LUCIA. Yeah, I don't want to talk about it anymore. Let's talk

about Crazy Pete and the loft party, or something. Because we're having a good time.
EUGENE. Yeah.
LUCIA. Are you?
EUGENE. Yeah, you? *(Lucia nods. They move closer together.)*
LUCIA. It's nice. *(They begin to kiss. They move passionately, touching each other's faces, necks, shoulders. Instinctively Eugene reaches up to undo the top button of Lucia's blouse. Lucia closes her eyes for a moment, letting him, then pulls away sharply.)* Wait — please — I'm not —
EUGENE. Oh God, I'm sorry.
LUCIA. No, it's all right. It's just this intense ... thing. And you have to be, ready.
EUGENE. I'm so sorry. I didn't ...
LUCIA. Maybe it doesn't matter, I don't know anymore. But I'm not sure if we can, it's maybe too ...
EUGENE. Yeah, I'm sorry.
LUCIA. It's late, anyway.
EUGENE. Yeah. Do you want me to stay? I mean I could go if you want or I could stay, and we could just ... stay.
LUCIA. I don't know, I've got treatment in the morning. So I guess I should get some sleep.
EUGENE. Yeah, okay. I'm really sorry.
LUCIA. No, it's okay, it's me. It's just ... whatever. I'll see you later?
EUGENE. Yeah ... goodnight. *(Eugene reluctantly exits.)*

Scene 6

The coffee shop. Milton sits at the table. Eugene enters, talking on his cell phone. He is leaving a message.

EUGENE. Hey, Lucia, it's me. I just ... I'm not sure why you're not calling me back, I just want to ... I think we should talk about everything. *(Crossing to Milton.)* Okay, call me. Hi Dad.
MILTON. Hello, hello. I think it's important that we're doing

this. Taking the time.

EUGENE. Yeah, sure.

MILTON. What's that? On your hand.

EUGENE. It's nothing. It's …

MILTON. You drew something, on your hand?

EUGENE. It's a tattoo. It's a tattoo. It's a …

MILTON. Yes, I see. A tattoo.

EUGENE. I don't want to talk about it. Right now.

MILTON. Well we can talk about it later, because it's not going anywhere, is it.

EUGENE. I know you know what a tattoo is. That's not … impressive.

MILTON. Fine. Fine. Did you read the clipping? The use of marijuana? I'm interested in your thoughts. Eager to wade, as it were, through the soup.

EUGENE. You know something, I can't do this right now. I really can't. I'm not in the mood.

MILTON. Is everything all right?

EUGENE. Not really. Not everything. Look, I'm just, there's things on my mind. Would you mind, could we … have lunch another time, or something. I'm just having, a bad week.

MILTON. Eugene, where are you going?

EUGENE. Let's just reschedule, okay.

MILTON. Eugene, please sit down.

EUGENE. I don't want to talk about the soup, or med school, or the trial. I don't want to talk about the questions, okay, I can't deal with the questions. I'm having a very bad week, okay.

MILTON. Okay, okay … and what kind of week am I having?

EUGENE. I don't know.

MILTON. What kind of mood am I in?

EUGENE. I don't know.

MILTON. That's right. You don't. Because you didn't ask me. So I'll tell you. I'm in the mood to have lunch. I'm also having a very bad week and I was really looking forward to today. In fact I wanted to ask for your help. So. Could you possibly sit down. *(Eugene hesitates and then sits down.)*

EUGENE. What kind of help?

MILTON. I was hoping you could renew my faith.

EUGENE. Your faith?
MILTON. In the questions.
EUGENE. I just told you …
MILTON. I said to myself: he is young, he's in school, he has energy and illusions. We'll have lunch.
EUGENE. What happened? Why was your week so bad?
MILTON. There's a six-year-old girl who can't stop coughing. There's also a woman who walks into my office and she looks exactly like your mother. Same eyes, same face. She has a head injury and can't remember anything. I call her Rachel by mistake — it just falls out of my mouth — and she looks up at me and asks: Is that my name? And then yesterday Mr. Rudolph appears to show me canvases that are dark and sad and full of pain. He tells me he has a tumor, and he has poured his anger into these canvases. The experience has been healing. For him. The canvases were supposed to be healing for other people. Is he selfish, this man, Rudolph Rudolph? Or can we only heal ourselves? The six-year-old girl has stopped coughing until she sees one of the canvases and then she starts crying, and the crying turns to coughing. That was my week. Tell me about yours.
EUGENE. Did you find out her real name, that woman?
MILTON. Her brother called me that afternoon. Samantha. But Rachel — it just fell out of my mouth.
EUGENE. It's just this clinical trial. Watching these people, and they're trying to make decisions, about their lives. And they want some kind of certainty …
MILTON. There's no certainty, that's what it means not to have a cure for something.
EUGENE. Right.
MILTON. You've got to remember that we all are constantly facing uncertainty. For example, at any time, any of us could in fact get hit by a bus. Or some such thing.
EUGENE. But nobody wants to talk about buses.
MILTON. It's true, it's not popular, people don't like to be reminded of the fundamental truth of buses.
EUGENE. I don't know how to renew anybody's faith.
MILTON. Well then, we'll just eat our lunch. *(He takes two take-out containers of soup out of a paper bag and hands one to Eugene.)*

Scene 7

Lucia's apartment. Juliet enters and places a piece in the mosaic. She exits as Lucia and Jeremy enter. Lucia is in pain.

JEREMY. Here we are. It's okay. God, do they always come on so suddenly, these headaches?
LUCIA. Yeah.
JEREMY. Can you take anything?
LUCIA. It doesn't help.
JEREMY. Maybe you should get some sleep?
LUCIA. No — I had this nightmare last night — you say you've been dreaming about my mom …
JEREMY. Yeah, sometimes.
LUCIA. Me too. There was this big house and she was all alone and she was in pain, her face was all twisted.
JEREMY. Don't say that, we don't know if it was like that.
LUCIA. No, we don't know anything, so I have to dream it.
JEREMY. I don't think she was alone. And I think she found some kind of peace.
LUCIA. Well that sounds nice, I wish I dreamed it like that. But I guess I'm too scared. So I just see her face all twisted.
JEREMY. You can't do that to yourself.
LUCIA. I was thinking — I woke up and I was thinking, what if you could find that town where she was, those last months. You could ask at the hospital in Paris, where she ended up, find out who brought her there, and you could find that town.
JEREMY. Why? It doesn't matter. Not right now. What matters is where you are, dealing with this thing, getting the best possible care. Where she was, that's in the past …
LUCIA. No, it's not —
JEREMY. You said you don't believe in ghosts.
LUCIA. They don't seem to care if you believe in them or not.
JEREMY. I just don't think it's a good idea, digging up old secrets.

51

People could get hurt.
LUCIA. What people?
JEREMY. We could. I mean that whole miserable time, when we were searching for her, I don't want to dig that up. Those choices.
LUCIA. We didn't make choices. We just looked. And failed.
JEREMY. I don't want to talk about this. It doesn't matter, none of it matters. Let's talk about it later, when you don't have this headache.
LUCIA. I'll have a different headache. I want to talk about it now.
JEREMY. What matters is what we do now. The present, and the future —
LUCIA. I told you already, stop talking to me about the future. And don't try to tell me what matters. You said you wanted to help me get through this.
JEREMY. I do.
LUCIA. So I'm asking you to do this one thing. Because I want to know where she was. If she was alone, if there was pain, if she cried, if there's any comfort, if she ever thought of me. I want to know where she was. Please. You say you think she found some kind of peace — I want to know if that's possible. If there's any such thing. I have to know that. When I wake up from these dreams, I have to know that.
JEREMY. I'm so sorry. I'm so —
LUCIA. Will you find out? Will you ask at the hospital in Paris?
JEREMY. Wait, listen —
LUCIA. Will you?
JEREMY. No.
LUCIA. Jesus, can't you do this for me, can't you —
JEREMY. No, wait — I won't ask at the hospital. Because I don't have to … Because I know where she was. And she wasn't alone and there was some pain, but there is such a thing as peace. I promise.
LUCIA. What are you talking about?
JEREMY. She used to sit in this garden. Up until the last day, she used to … it smells like honeysuckle …
LUCIA. What are you saying?
JEREMY. I was looking for her, that whole time, remember, I was supposed to figure out where she was …
LUCIA. But you couldn't. Because you can't find somebody who doesn't want to be found. You kept saying that, remember.
JEREMY. But I did find her.

LUCIA. No, because you told me —
JEREMY. I'm telling you, right now I'm telling you ... somehow, finally, I got in touch with her. And we spoke on the phone. I said we would postpone the wedding, come to see her. And she begged me — She said don't say anything, stay where you are and let my daughter have her wedding. And she'll remember me from before. And she can imagine me maybe at the wedding. Dancing maybe. If she never sees me like this, then she can still imagine, that I was ... she said I beg you. I am very sick, and I am begging you. This is what I want.
LUCIA. She never said that. She never ...
JEREMY. Please. I want you to forgive us.
LUCIA. Us? You lied to me? How many fucking years have you been lying to me. Us? You can't do that. You can't make that kind of choice for somebody. I never got to say goodbye. What the fuck gives you the right to make that kind of choice for somebody?
JEREMY. Choice? When she said that — I am begging you? She said this is what I want. I am very sick and this is what I want.
LUCIA. Yeah? Well guess what. Guess who's very sick now and guess what she wants.
JEREMY. Wait —
LUCIA. I want you to go. Go back to Paris or wherever and find somebody else's life to fuck with.
JEREMY. Wait — I have to tell you. You want to know where she was. I went there, not long after she died. To the town, it's called Rochelle. There's a woman, Therese, she took care of your mother, she stayed at her side. So she wasn't alone. There's a garden, it smells like honeysuckle. Therese said your mother found her peace in the end, she did find a kind of ... and she was thinking of you. She had something for you, a wedding present. But she never sent it, so Therese kept it and gave it to me wrapped in newspaper. I've kept it all this time, but I don't know what it is, I never opened it. I can send it to you, is that what you want?
LUCIA. I want you to go. I want to be alone.
JEREMY. What are you going to do?
LUCIA. Make a list of who not to trust.
JEREMY. I'm so sorry. I'm so ... I'll call you, okay, later. Are you going to be okay?

LUCIA. Whatever. *(Jeremy exits. Juliet enters, carrying a package wrapped in newspaper.)*
JULIET. Five people never to trust. Number five.
LUCIA. Don't. Because I can't ...
JULIET. Doctors.
LUCIA. You didn't talk to doctors.
JULIET. Your mother. Your husband. And anybody else that wants to touch you.
LUCIA. I don't make lists.
JULIET. Yourself. That's number one.
LUCIA. Why do you always count backwards?
JULIET. Good question.
LUCIA. Let me guess.
JULIET. So you know when it's over. *(Juliet moves to the background, as Eugene enters and crosses to Lucia. Juliet watches, ignored by Lucia.)*
EUGENE. Hey, I got your message. Is everything okay?
LUCIA. Sure.
EUGENE. I tried calling you last night, a bunch of times. You weren't answering I guess.
LUCIA. I guess not.
EUGENE. Your message sounded a little ... upset.
LUCIA. What's on your hand? You have my bird on your hand?
EUGENE. It's not yours.
LUCIA. What's that for?
EUGENE. Inspiration.
LUCIA. Well I hope it works.
EUGENE. Are you okay?
LUCIA. Maybe I have a headache, what do you think?
EUGENE. Did you take anything? Did the pot help?
LUCIA. Do you think it's a headache?
EUGENE. What do you mean?
LUCIA. I guess that depends. On which drug I'm taking and the various side effects. I guess that's private information.
EUGENE. I'm not sure where you're going with this.
LUCIA. I guess somebody knows, somewhere in some file. Whether it's really a headache, and what happens next. Too bad it's none of my business.
EUGENE. Lucia, this whole question you have, about the

headaches and the various drug … possibilities, I really think you should talk to Dr. Slogan.

LUCIA. I don't want to talk about various possibilities, I want to talk about various actualities. I want your help.

EUGENE. I told you, the other night, I can't do that. What you're asking, it's not possible.

LUCIA. Did you have a good time, the other night?

EUGENE. Yes.

LUCIA. But then you left.

EUGENE. Because you asked me to.

LUCIA. Because it got complicated. I'm tired of complicated. I just want answers. Because there's nothing I can trust.

EUGENE. You can trust me.

LUCIA. Can I? Then give me answers.

EUGENE. That's not trust.

LUCIA. It's knowledge. The power of knowledge, isn't that what you said, why you wanted to be a doctor. To help people, because you care about them.

EUGENE. Why are you doing this? Twisting everything all around. Putting me in this … position. I mean what's going on? Did I miss something here? Did I miss the part where you decided to fuck with me?

LUCIA. Wait — I'm not —

EUGENE. Take the kid to Coney Island and maybe he'll pull some strings. Is that what's been going on here?

LUCIA. That's not —

EUGENE. I mean what's going on here?

LUCIA. I don't know.

EUGENE. Yeah, me neither. But it's bullshit to pretend it's about knowledge, or answers. Because you know it's not.

LUCIA. There are certain things that cannot happen at a time like this. Maybe you want them to and maybe you think they can, but they can't.

EUGENE. Says who.

LUCIA. Says lots of things. Number one headaches. For starters. Number two …

EUGENE. I thought you didn't make lists.

LUCIA. Well maybe I'm learning. I started wrong anyhow, you're supposed to count backwards, 54321.

EUGENE. Why is that?

LUCIA. So you know when to stop. When you hit zero.

EUGENE. Did we?

LUCIA. I did. And the thing about zero, it's just this big empty space and you can't take anybody with you.

EUGENE. Are you sure?

LUCIA. You're sure you won't help me.

EUGENE. I can't.

LUCIA. Well. Okay.

EUGENE. Okay?

LUCIA. 54321. And then you have to stop. Because we didn't meet at Pete's, at some crazy loft, you know. So it's not going to be okay, not today or next week. Because we can't, I can't, do it. So please, if you could …

EUGENE. If I could …

LUCIA. Go. If you could go. Please.

EUGENE. Okay. I guess … okay. But please call me, if you need anything. Or whatever.

LUCIA. Yeah. Okay. *(They look at each other, hesitating. Lucia turns away. Eugene exits. Lucia covers her face with her hands. Juliet crosses to Lucia.)*

JULIET. Okay. Let's go. Are you ready?

LUCIA. What are you doing?

JULIET. I think it's time to leave town.

LUCIA. No, you can't do this —

JULIET. Do you feel ready?

LUCIA. I don't feel anything. Is this what you call peace?

JULIET. Three things to pack before you go. Number three, plane ticket.

LUCIA. I want to know what peace feels like.

JULIET. Number two, your phrase book. Number one, you should take your wedding present. *(She holds out the package, wrapped in newspaper.)* I kept it safe for you. *(Lucia takes the present and throws it to the floor. The sound of breaking glass.)*

LUCIA. … Tell me what peace feels like.

JULIET. … I can't.

LUCIA. I needed you. *(Lucia walks away from Juliet.)*

56

JULIET. … Je suis désolée.
LUCIA. *(Turning back.)* What does that mean?
JULIET. It's in the phrase book. It means, don't you remember —
LUCIA. Tell me what it means.
JULIET. It means I'm sorry. *(Lucia breaks down. Juliet goes to her, bringing her the broken pieces.)*
LUCIA. It's all smashed into pieces.
JULIET. Well I guess we're lucky then. *(She gestures towards the mosaic.)* That you know what to do with those. *(She holds out the broken pieces to Lucia. Lucia takes them.)*

Scene 8

The coffee shop. Milton enters and sits at a table. Lucia enters and crosses to him.

LUCIA. Excuse me, are you … Milton?
MILTON. Yes, Lucia?
LUCIA. Hi. I'm sorry I'm a little late. I've had a lot going on.
MILTON. I realize that. And I do appreciate you calling me back.
LUCIA. I almost didn't. But your messages, I found them intriguing. I mean Rudolph Rudolph …
MILTON. I just found out his middle name is Lewis.
LUCIA. You made me laugh, which is impressive, right now.
MILTON. Aah, good. Well, I'm anxious to hear about this mosaic my son mentioned.
LUCIA. How is he? I haven't really … spoken to him.
MILTON. Yes, well, he's all right. He was glad that you were willing to meet with me. He felt that this piece you've been working on might be the kind of thing we're looking for.
LUCIA. Well, I don't know. I'm not finished with it yet — I've been working pretty much round the clock these past few days. But here's some of my other work. *(She shows him a portfolio.)*
MILTON. Aah yes, these look very interesting. Beautiful.

LUCIA. Thank you.

MILTON. It's for the hospital, like I said in my message. I'm interested in this notion that art could inspire a kind of healing.

LUCIA. Well I don't know about that.

MILTON. Neither do I. But it's an exciting possibility, wouldn't you say?

LUCIA. Yeah, I guess it is.

MILTON. I look forward to seeing the new mosaic, when it's finished.

LUCIA. Yes, of course.

MILTON. We would also be interested in seeing more new material, if you wanted to consider this an ongoing relationship.

LUCIA. A what?

MILTON. We might want to commission additional mosaics. If that would interest you.

LUCIA. That might be nice.

MILTON. I have a message, actually, from Eugene. He'd very much like to see you. He says he has something important to tell you, but he can talk to you about it at Coney Island tomorrow.

LUCIA. We're not, I wasn't going to Coney Island.

MILTON. He says he'll bring the car by at five. He's renting a car.

LUCIA. Why?

MILTON. The subway takes too fucking long. That's a quote.

LUCIA. Well tell him, tell him I don't know if I can go to Coney Island.

MILTON. The thing is … I've got a pretty hectic day, and I'm not sure I can reach him. So you should probably call him yourself, if you need to … discuss anything.

LUCIA. Right. Right. How convenient.

MILTON. Well. It's very nice to meet you, Lucia. I look forward to seeing this mosaic. I think it takes great vision, to be an artist.

LUCIA. You think?

MILTON. I mean I imagine you feel lost sometimes with all of these ideas and images all around you, like you're in the middle of some, some …

LUCIA. Soup?

MILTON. I was going to say storm. Eugene mentioned the soup, did he. I was going to say storm, with all these possibilities rush-

ing around you. And you have to find your focus. I look at a piece of work like this, and I'm not sure how you do it.
LUCIA. Neither am I. That's the big secret.
MILTON. I've had a lot of days like that, recently. And years ago, when my wife got sick, there were so many times, I thought, I can't be this thing, this doctor, who pretends to understand everything. And then I would drive to work and put on the coat, and the day would begin. And then a few weeks later you catch yourself in the mirror and you think, look at that, I'm still a doctor.
LUCIA. Yeah, there's that glimpse in the mirror —
MILTON. And there you are. In the storm.

Scene 10

Coney Island. The sounds of a boardwalk. Lucia and Eugene enter.

LUCIA. Why did you bring me here?
EUGENE. It's the last day of the season. The rides and everything are going to shut down. So I thought we should come back before that happened. Are you sorry you came?
LUCIA. No, I'm not sorry. It's good to see you.
EUGENE. Yeah?
LUCIA. Yeah.
EUGENE. Also we're on an important mission, to get the sloth. Because the octopus is lonely.
LUCIA. How would you know, the octopus is at my place.
EUGENE. I think that was my point.
LUCIA. … It was funny, meeting your dad. He wants to commission more of my work, for the hospital. Do you know how that feels? I'm excited, I can't help it, I feel excited. So — thanks.
EUGENE. Okay.
LUCIA. He said — your dad — he said you had something to tell me. What does that mean?

EUGENE. It means I decided. I'm going to go into the computer at the hospital tomorrow, to find out about your treatment. Which drugs.
LUCIA. You are?
EUGENE. Yeah.
LUCIA. But you said you couldn't. That it would compromise everything.
EUGENE. Yeah, well it will. But there's got to be somebody you can trust. And the thing is I want to be that person. Because I can't get you out of my mind. So there we are. Fuck the trial.
LUCIA. Wait — don't say that.
EUGENE. What.
LUCIA. Fuck the trial —
EUGENE. We have to take responsibility, for what we're doing.
LUCIA. I don't know what trust is anymore.
EUGENE. Just tell me if you want me to do it. I don't want to, but I will. If you really believe knowing will make this easier … Do you want me to do it?
LUCIA. I don't know.
EUGENE. What do you want?
LUCIA. I want to know what happens next.
EUGENE. … Hey, do you — do you want to go on The Cyclone? The roller coaster. Can we do that?
LUCIA. Right now? I don't really feel like it.
EUGENE. I know. I know you don't. But just one thing, like I told you, it's the last weekend, so the rides are shutting down after tonight. So it's up to you, but otherwise we're talking next year.
LUCIA. Next year.
EUGENE. Yeah. So what do you say, roller coaster?
LUCIA. … Okay.
EUGENE. Yeah? *(He takes her hand and begins leading her offstage. She hesitates a moment and then:)*
LUCIA. Here we go … *(They rush offstage. The sound of a wooden roller coaster. The stage is suddenly lit with Christmas lights flowing up and down in the shape of a roller coaster. The rest of the lights fade as the carnival music begins.)*

End of Play

PROPERTY LIST

Seashells (LUCIA)
Carousel horse figurine (JULIET)
Mug with pencils (EUGENE)
Cigarettes, lighter (REENA)
Phrase book (JEREMY)
Glasses of champagne (LUCIA)
Paperwork (EUGENE)
Papers (LUCIA)
Newspaper clipping (MILTON)
Form (EUGENE)
Rolled-up Picasso print (EUGENE)
Book (EUGENE)
Napkin, pen (LUCIA)
Picnic basket (JEREMY)
Orange stuffed octopus (EUGENE)
Books (EUGENE)
Wig in a box (JULIET)
Baseball cap (LUCIA)
Clippers (LUCIA)
Bananas (JEREMY)
Pipe (EUGENE)
Cranberry juice, glass (LUCIA)
Orange stuffed octopus wearing wig (LUCIA)
Cell phone (EUGENE)
Two containers of soup in a paper bag (MILTON)
Package wrapped in newspaper (JULIET)
Pieces of broken glass (JULIET)
Portfolio (LUCIA)

SOUND EFFECTS

Carnival music
Loud rock music
Phone rings
Breaking glass
Boardwalk sounds
Roller coaster